This workbook belongs to

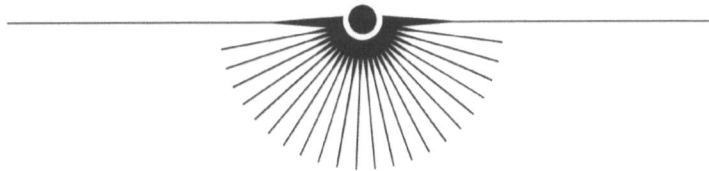

Daily Alignment Workbook

To request permissions, contact the publisher at freedomhousepublishingco@gmail.com or support@mrsveronicaanne.com

Paperback: 978-1-952566-16-5

Printed in the USA.

Freedom House Publishing Co

Middleton, ID 83644

www.freedomhousepublishingco.com

How to use this workbook

I'm so glad you have chosen to enter into this practice! I honor you and your choice to be willing to do this work. As you commit to yourself and this practice, you will start to see small changes and improvements the first week. This book is half workbook, half journal.

The prompts are all designed to help you do the following:
- Make lasting, positive changes.
- Build a better relationship with God.
- Be a better friend to yourself.
- Live in a state of gratitude.
- Listen to your higher self.
- Change negative core beliefs.
- Nourish your physical, mental, and spiritual self.
- Have a higher and more stable amount of peace.

The workbook can be used alone but is designed to be a daily support for my transformation program. It will help you put systems in place by focusing on the small, daily habits because that is where true change happens. You can set goals or have a vision board to map where you are going, but **systems** are the way to achieve what you are hoping for, while growing happiness daily. They are what outlive the goals. Your system facilitates and maintains your growth and progress—no more two steps forward and one step back. You will hold your ground. That territory is hard won! Using this workbook every day will help you navigate life better, especially the hard things.

I recommend *not* trying to implement all actions on the first day. Being overwhelmed can lead to burnout and then abandonment. Pick something to start with and be faithful at implementing it into your routine. Once it becomes automatic or easy to maintain, add one or two more. The small victories will feed on each other. The momentum will be addicting!

MORNING:

Set a time - Pick a time early in the morning and keep this appointment time with yourself and God <u>no matter what!</u> I recommend around five in the morning. There are plenty of studies and evidence to support the benefit of waking early and the success that almost always follows those who are consistent. Yes, waking up early might be hard for you, but the benefits you will start to experience will far outweigh any of the so-called "sacrifices." You will start to relish these morning meetings and it will feel like a treat—because it is—instead of an inconvenience. Wake up in the morning, grab your workbook, and go to your sacred space or meditation spot. This can be a dedicated space for you or simply a room you can be alone in, uninterrupted. Do not stop to look at your phone! When you first wake up your brain waves are primed for inspiration and receiving. If you start scrolling through your phone, you're going to move into different brainwaves and they're going to work against you. It will also kick on your automatic subconscious programming and you might miss this amazing appointment all together! Once in your spot, do a a quick stretch. his is not to get your heart rate going; it is just to get you awake enough to do your morning alignment. In fact, I recommend not exercising before meditation, because it can make it hard for you to relax enough for a deep meditation. I teach the Alignment Method as a preparation for prayer. It puts your body in a relaxed state so it is easier to commune with God.

Pray- It's really easy to pray for the same thing every day, or to make a quick, half-hearted effort in our prayers. I want you to stop and think, however, that the creator of the sun, the moon, and the stars wants to have a conversation with you! It's an amazing gift and because it's so freely given, it's easy to overlook. I added this prayer prompt so you might take a moment to think before you pray to make a list of the things you really want to talk to your Father about and include the people you want to make sure you pray for. Planned prayers are more effective prayers.

Read Scripture - This is one of the best ways to worship God. You can learn about His character, how much He loves you, His plans for you, and how to communicate with Him. It helps you hear His voice. Memorizing scripture or thinking deeply on a scripture are ways to ingrain His words in you. He'll help you understand on a deeper level. I occasionally use a quote as well. Sometimes I work on the same scripture for days or even a couple weeks. Memorizing or pondering deeply on a verse will allow His words to become part of you. Pick a scripture or story to focus on and suck the marrow out of it.

Design your day - This workbook is not a planner and this prompt is not a to-do list, but it is a place to write what you are intending for the day. How do you want to show up for yourself today? How do you want to show up for others? What are you going to do to move a bit closer to becoming the person you want to become? Write it here. Consider praying about it. He may have something to add! At the end of the day you can report back to the Lord.

Meditate - Meditation makes everything better. It makes you smarter, makes you feel younger and less stressed, and more in tune with yourself and God, to name just a few of the benefits. This prompt is for any insights you may receive while doing your meditation practice. Starting your day with a reminder of your divinity, removing any stress, and thoughtfully planning your day are great ways to live with intention and meditation can provide that.

Meditation helps you grab hold of your day and run your life rather than letting it run you. I have the *Alignment Method for Meditation* course that will teach you how to fully take advantage of this amazing practice that can be life changing.

Identify Beliefs/Patterns - When you notice any action, belief, or pattern you want to change, write it here. You can write several just to make a list, but it is most effective if you only try and tackle one or two at a time. Awareness is half the battle with . . . well almost anything. Once you are aware, you can begin making changes!

Write an Affirmation - This is directly connected to your prompt of what you are wanting to change. It generally is any statement that begins to undo what your negative beliefs and patterns are. It should be something that resonates with you and makes you feel empowered to change. If you feel you are ugly or fat, you may not resonate with the statement, "I am beautiful." You may like statements of truth like, "I am created in the image of Heavenly Mother." Or you can put a hand on your heart and a hand on your middle and simply thank your body for performing as well as it has for you. You can work your way to, "I am beautiful and I love you just as you are."

EVENING:

At the end of the day, take a few minutes and complete the second page of the prompts. You will find that as you continue to do this, your mind will be looking for answers to these questions as you go throughout your day. They will become easier to answer and you will begin to change. Such a simple thing, yet so profound.

Meditate – Again, in the afternoon or evening, spend about 20 minutes meditating. You might think you don't have time for this, but it will actually make you more efficient and the unloading of the stress will help you sleep better.

Honor yourself - This can be something as simple as scheduling a coaching/therapy/doctor appointment you've been avoiding, or taking a bath. Maybe you showed up as you were wanting to with your husband or kids. Any action you are taking that honors your highest self or when you are acting from your highest self, write it here.

Connect with God – What did you do today to feel connected with God? If you're struggling with this, step away from the lights and the noise and go find Him. Go for a hike, sit in a sacred space, or just quiet yourself and listen. Recognize that effort by writing here.

Recognize God's Hand – What happened today that is evidence of God's personal interest in you? Maybe it's something small. Maybe you were able to have a needed conversation or you see where He intervened on your behalf to prevent a mistake. Or maybe you received an answer to a nagging question, or something to increase your faith. The more intentional you are about looking for this, the more you will find evidence that He is intimately involved in your life.

Identify Something Done Well – What did you do well today? It's so easy to focus on where we fell short, but we often do things well. Take a moment and pull something out of your day that you feel you did a good job on. Maybe you said something loving to your child, did a great job at work, or cooked a great dinner. It doesn't have to be something big. Just give yourself credit for the times you are awesome!

Remember – Life goes by so quickly. Write down anything you want to remember from the day—maybe a beautiful sunset, or something silly your child said. Anything you want to take a mental picture of should be written here. It's a mini-journal moment.

Visualize – Everything is spiritually created before it is physically created. Spiritually create yourself and your life, then take it to the Lord. Start visualizing your future self, the more detailed the better. Your brain doesn't know the difference between reality and what it is visualizing. So, you can create new habits by creating a clear picture in your mind of the results you are wanting. For example, if you are wanting to respond differently to your kids, you visualize yourself doing just that, over and over. That is just a small thing you can use visualization for. It is equally great for helping you become the person you want to be. Visualizing at the end of meditation or when going to sleep is an especially effective use of this tool. You are utilizing the theta brain waves and can make changes at a quicker pace when visualizing in this state, because you are affecting your thoughts at a subconscious level.

Create your Future Self – This is connected to visualizing. The more clear we get and the more detailed the picture, the more likely it is you will become the person you want to be. What does that future person look like? How do people feel around her? How does she treat others? What does she wear? What does her house look like? When you think about your future self, how do you feel? Fall in love with her. This practice will help you choose moments to show up as that future self until those moments become more consistent and you ARE her. (Hint: People are most guilty of not dreaming big enough. Consider asking God to help you see not only how amazing you are, but how amazing you can become. Let the first thoughts of your greatness stick. Don't talk yourself down to something smaller!)

Express Gratitude – Write a few things you are grateful for every day. Start with three and try to not write the same thing twice. The more you do this, the more you will find to be grateful for and you will begin to live in a state of abundance. This has positive impacts on your brain, your emotions, and therefore, your life. When we feel grateful, we eliminate feelings of negativity and lacking, envy, and resentment. We feel more peace, more joy, and more satisfaction with our life. Who doesn't want that?

Nourish your body – Plan out what you are going to eat today to feel good. Planning out what you are going to eat in the morning helps you make better decisions throughout the day so you don't choose foods at the last minute that rob you of your energy.

This is *your* workbook. You can leave something blank, or fill it in the way helps you most. There are also pages in the back to use how you like. This sacred time is when I often have states of "flow" and I have a lot of information pouring through me quickly. If your thoughts are spilling off your page, don't worry; there's room in the back to catch all those insights.

Do this workbook every day and you will begin to live more and more in alignment with God and with your higher self. Filling out the workbook may seem like a lot, but after a few days, I found that I was able to fill out the prompts (most days) in about five to ten minutes. It's such a great investment in yourself and your family because **self-care is family-care**. Changing yourself for the better changes your family for the better. You show up differently in all the best ways.

Nearly everyone wants to elevate their lives to greater peace, joy, and contentment, but not everyone is willing to take action on the roots that affect the growth. Purchasing this workbook shows you are willing to do the work. This workbook will help you take the steps to nourish your efforts. I promise you peace will multiply along with the results of your efforts. Just start. Take a single step in the direction you are wanting to go; do one thing to move you closer, then keep doing it. It really is that simple. Take all the new things you are learning and now *implement* them. As you keep promises to yourself, you will be living in integrity to who you are and who you want to be. If needed, decrease an expectation to guarantee that you can perform it 100%. Small daily acts bring about great changes.

Keep this workbook as a record of your progress and growth. You can, and should, review all the insights and things you feel called to do.

DAILY ALIGNMENT

MORNING

DATE TODAY:

- ☒ Stretch
- ☒ Meditate
- ☒ Pray
- ☒ Scriptures
- ☐ Exercise

TODAY I AM GOING
TO NOURISH MY
BODY WITH
- Blender Muffin
- Salad
- Juice
- Beans & walnut
  tacos

WHAT I AM PRAYING FOR

I am praying for help to forgive my brother

MEDITATION INSIGHTS

I am good at recognizing shame and how it feels
in my body

THE SCRIPTURE I AM LETTING SINK INTO ME IS

"The inner critic is actually an outside voice that has
been internalized as your own"
                    -Dr. Nicole Le Pera

MY DESIGN FOR MY DAY IS

Keep promises to myself the whole day. Do all my
self care items today as a priority.

**THE ACTION/BELIEF/PATTERN I AM WORKING TO
CHANGE IS**

Self Care is selfish.

TODAY'S AFFIRMATION

Self care is family-care.
when I eliminate negativity from my own life, I do not pass it to
my family.

mrs.veronica anne

DAILY ALIGNMENT

EVENING

DATE TODAY:

☐ Meditate

☒ Report back to God

☒ Visualize

I FEEL GRATEFUL FOR:

- The Sunset

- Lunch with friends

- Heartfelt conversation with my son.

TODAY I HONORED MYSELF BY

I made an appointment with a coach who helped me with my issues around business

TODAY I CONNECTED WITH GOD BY

I took few minutes while waiting at school pickup to talk to God and re-center myself.

I SAW GOD'S HAND IN MY LIFE TODAY WHEN

The most beautiful sunset.

SOMETHING I DID WELL TODAY IS

I caught myself saying really negative things to myself I stopped and put a hand on my heart & apologized.

SOMETHING I WANT TO REMEMBER FROM TODAY

The feeling of progress I am making towards being a better friend to myself.

SOMETHING ABOUT MY FUTURE SELF IS

She doesn't need the approval of others. She stays true to herself.

IT IS A DENIAL OF THE DIVINITY WITHIN US TO DOUBT OUR POTENTIAL AND OUR POSSIBILITIES. - JAMES E. FAUST

mrs.veronica anne

DAILY ALIGNMENT

MORNING

DATE TODAY:

☒ Stretch

☒ Meditate

☒ Pray

☒ Scriptures

☒ Exercise

TODAY I AM GOING
TO NOURISH MY
BODY WITH

- Green smoothie
- Salad
- Apple & Almond butter
- Tofu fried rice

WHAT I AM PRAYING FOR

Aunt Nora- Her Cancer
my country
help with my test

MEDITATION INSIGHTS

My problem in trusting others is rooted in me not
trusting myself. I trust God fully.

THE SCRIPTURE I AM LETTING SINK INTO ME IS

"The LORD hath anointed me to preach good tidings
unto the meek; he hath sent me to bind up the
brokenhearted, to proclaim liberty to the captives,
and the opening of the prison to them that are bound;"

Isaiah 61:1

MY DESIGN FOR MY DAY IS

Show up with love to those around me.

**THE ACTION/BELIEF/PATTERN I AM WORKING TO
CHANGE IS**

I have to carry my burdens myself.

TODAY'S AFFIRMATION

Help is available to me.
I can trust God to fight my battles for me.

mrs.veronica anne

DAILY ALIGNMENT

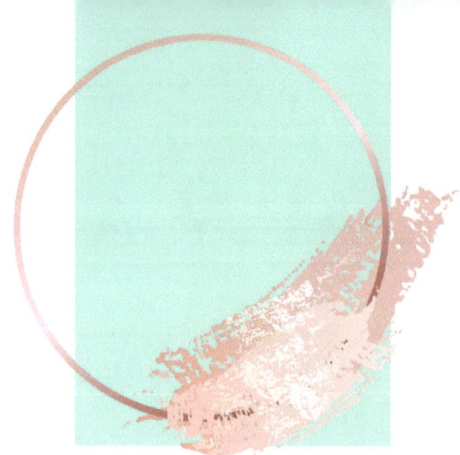

EVENING

DATE TODAY:

☒ Meditate

☒ Report back to God

☒ Visualize

I FEEL GRATEFUL FOR:

- Finding the missing check
- Insight into how to deal with a problem I'm having with my son
- Time with my kids today

TODAY I HONORED MYSELF BY

Setting a new boundary.
I will not yell and I will not allow
for others to yell at me.

TODAY I CONNECTED WITH GOD BY

Going for a hike

I SAW GOD'S HAND IN MY LIFE TODAY WHEN

I realized that if I had not lost my old job, I would
Never have found my current job that fits me so
much better.

SOMETHING I DID WELL TODAY IS

Ran all my errands and made myself an awesome
dinner.

SOMETHING I WANT TO REMEMBER FROM TODAY

One my hike today, I felt God gave me clear
instructions about how to help my son.

SOMETHING ABOUT MY FUTURE SELF IS

She is a cheerleader of those around her

IT IS A DENIAL OF THE DIVINITY WITHIN US TO DOUBT OUR POTENTIAL
AND OUR POSSIBILITIES. - JAMES E. FAUST

You do not rise
to the level of your goals,
you fall to
the level of your
systems.

-James Clear

DAILY ALIGNMENT

MORNING

DATE TODAY:

☐ Stretch

☐ Meditate

☐ Pray

☐ Scriptures

☐ Exercise

TODAY I AM GOING
TO NOURISH MY
BODY WITH

_____

_____

_____

_____

WHAT I AM PRAYING FOR

_____
_____
_____

MEDITATION INSIGHTS

_____
_____
_____

THE SCRIPTURE I AM LETTING SINK INTO ME IS

_____
_____
_____

MY DESIGN FOR MY DAY IS

_____
_____
_____

THE ACTION/BELIEF/PATTERN I AM WORKING TO CHANGE IS

_____
_____
_____

TODAY'S AFFIRMATION

DAILY ALIGNMENT

EVENING

DATE TODAY:

☐ Meditate

☐ Report back to God

☐ Visualize

I FEEL GRATEFUL FOR:

TODAY I HONORED MYSELF BY

_____

_____

_____

TODAY I CONNECTED WITH GOD BY

_____

_____

_____

I SAW GOD'S HAND IN MY LIFE TODAY WHEN

_____

_____

SOMETHING I DID WELL TODAY IS

_____

_____

SOMETHING I WANT TO REMEMBER FROM TODAY

_____

_____

SOMETHING ABOUT MY FUTURE SELF IS

_____

_____

_____

IT IS A DENIAL OF THE DIVINITY WITHIN US TO DOUBT OUR POTENTIAL AND OUR POSSIBILITIES. - JAMES E. FAUST

DAILY ALIGNMENT

MORNING

DATE TODAY:

☐ Stretch

☐ Meditate

☐ Pray

☐ Scriptures

☐ Exercise

TODAY I AM GOING
TO NOURISH MY
BODY WITH

_____

_____

_____

WHAT I AM PRAYING FOR

_____

_____

_____

MEDITATION INSIGHTS

_____

_____

_____

THE SCRIPTURE I AM LETTING SINK INTO ME IS

_____

_____

_____

MY DESIGN FOR MY DAY IS

_____

_____

_____

THE ACTION/BELIEF/PATTERN I AM WORKING TO CHANGE IS

_____

_____

_____

TODAY'S AFFIRMATION

DAILY ALIGNMENT

EVENING

DATE TODAY:

☐ Meditate

☐ Report back
   to God

☐ Visualize

**I FEEL GRATEFUL
FOR:**

TODAY I HONORED MYSELF BY

_____
_____
_____

TODAY I CONNECTED WITH GOD BY

_____
_____
_____

I SAW GOD'S HAND IN MY LIFE TODAY WHEN

_____
_____

SOMETHING I DID WELL TODAY IS

_____
_____
_____

SOMETHING I WANT TO REMEMBER FROM TODAY

_____
_____

SOMETHING ABOUT MY FUTURE SELF IS

_____
_____
_____

"CONTINUOUS EFFORT – NOT STRENGTH OR INTELLIGENCE – IS THE KEY
TO UNLOCKING OUR POTENTIAL." – LIANE CARDES

mrs.veronica anne

DAILY ALIGNMENT

MORNING

DATE TODAY:

☐ Stretch

☐ Meditate

☐ Pray

☐ Scriptures

☐ Exercise

TODAY I AM GOING
TO NOURISH MY
BODY WITH

_____

_____

_____

WHAT I AM PRAYING FOR

_____

_____

_____

MEDITATION INSIGHTS

_____

_____

_____

THE SCRIPTURE I AM LETTING SINK INTO ME IS

_____

_____

_____

MY DESIGN FOR MY DAY IS

_____

_____

THE ACTION/BELIEF/PATTERN I AM WORKING TO CHANGE IS

_____

_____

_____

TODAY'S AFFIRMATION

DAILY ALIGNMENT

EVENING

DATE TODAY:

☐ Meditate

☐ Report back
   to God

☐ Visualize

**I FEEL GRATEFUL
FOR:**

TODAY I HONORED MYSELF BY

_____
_____
_____

TODAY I CONNECTED WITH GOD BY

_____
_____
_____

I SAW GOD'S HAND IN MY LIFE TODAY WHEN

_____
_____
_____

SOMETHING I DID WELL TODAY IS

_____
_____
_____

SOMETHING I WANT TO REMEMBER FROM TODAY

_____
_____
_____

SOMETHING ABOUT MY FUTURE SELF IS

_____
_____
_____

IF WE DID ALL THE THINGS WE ARE CAPABLE OF,
WE WOULD LITERALLY ASTOUND OURSELVES. -THOMAS EDISON

DAILY ALIGNMENT

MORNING

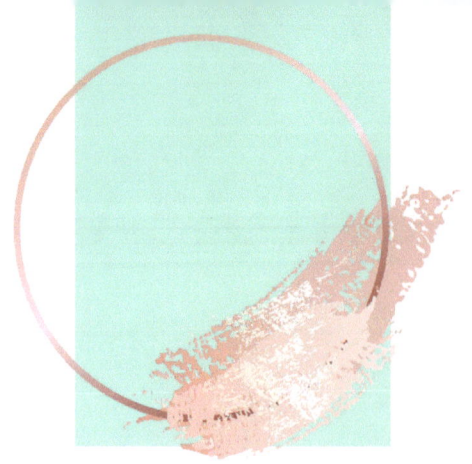

DATE TODAY:

☐ Stretch

☐ Meditate

☐ Pray

☐ Scriptures

☐ Exercise

TODAY I AM GOING
TO NOURISH MY
BODY WITH

_____

_____

_____

WHAT I AM PRAYING FOR

_____

_____

_____

MEDITATION INSIGHTS

_____

_____

_____

THE SCRIPTURE I AM LETTING SINK INTO ME IS

_____

_____

_____

MY DESIGN FOR MY DAY IS

_____

_____

_____

THE ACTION/BELIEF/PATTERN I AM WORKING TO CHANGE IS

_____

_____

_____

TODAY'S AFFIRMATION

DAILY ALIGNMENT

EVENING

DATE TODAY:

☐ Meditate

☐ Report back
  to God

☐ Visualize

**I FEEL GRATEFUL
FOR:**

TODAY I HONORED MYSELF BY

_____
_____
_____

TODAY I CONNECTED WITH GOD BY

_____
_____
_____

I SAW GOD'S HAND IN MY LIFE TODAY WHEN

_____
_____
_____

SOMETHING I DID WELL TODAY IS

_____
_____

SOMETHING I WANT TO REMEMBER FROM TODAY

_____
_____

SOMETHING ABOUT MY FUTURE SELF IS

_____
_____
_____

GOD NEVER LOSES SIGHT OF OUR ETERNAL POTENTIAL,
EVEN WHEN WE DO. - CAROLE M. STEPHENS

"Be patient with yourself. Self-growth is tender; it's holy ground. There's no greater investment."

-Stephen Covey

DAILY ALIGNMENT

MORNING

DATE TODAY:

☐ Stretch

☐ Meditate

☐ Pray

☐ Scriptures

☐ Exercise

TODAY I AM GOING
TO NOURISH MY
BODY WITH

_____

_____

_____

WHAT I AM PRAYING FOR

_____

_____

_____

MEDITATION INSIGHTS

_____

_____

_____

THE SCRIPTURE I AM LETTING SINK INTO ME IS

_____

_____

_____

MY DESIGN FOR MY DAY IS

_____

_____

**THE ACTION/BELIEF/PATTERN I AM WORKING TO
CHANGE IS**

_____

_____

_____

TODAY'S AFFIRMATION

DAILY ALIGNMENT

EVENING

DATE TODAY:

☐ Meditate

☐ Report back
   to God

☐ Visualize

**I FEEL GRATEFUL
FOR:**

TODAY I HONORED MYSELF BY

_____
_____
_____

TODAY I CONNECTED WITH GOD BY

_____
_____
_____

I SAW GOD'S HAND IN MY LIFE TODAY WHEN

_____
_____
_____

SOMETHING I DID WELL TODAY IS

_____
_____
_____

SOMETHING I WANT TO REMEMBER FROM TODAY

_____
_____
_____

SOMETHING ABOUT MY FUTURE SELF IS

_____
_____
_____

YOU'RE NOT INTIMIDATING. THEY ARE INTIMIDATED.
THERE IS A BIG DIFFERENCE.

mrs.veronica anne

DAILY ALIGNMENT

MORNING

DATE TODAY:

☐ Stretch

☐ Meditate

☐ Pray

☐ Scriptures

☐ Exercise

WHAT I AM PRAYING FOR

_____
_____
_____

MEDITATION INSIGHTS

_____
_____
_____

THE SCRIPTURE I AM LETTING SINK INTO ME IS

_____
_____
_____

TODAY I AM GOING
TO NOURISH MY
BODY WITH

_____
_____
_____
_____

MY DESIGN FOR MY DAY IS

_____
_____
_____

THE ACTION/BELIEF/PATTERN I AM WORKING TO CHANGE IS

_____
_____
_____

TODAY'S AFFIRMATION

DAILY ALIGNMENT

EVENING

DATE TODAY:

☐ Meditate

☐ Report back
   to God

☐ Visualize

**I FEEL GRATEFUL
FOR:**

TODAY I HONORED MYSELF BY

_____
_____
_____

TODAY I CONNECTED WITH GOD BY

_____
_____
_____

I SAW GOD'S HAND IN MY LIFE TODAY WHEN

_____
_____
_____

SOMETHING I DID WELL TODAY IS

_____
_____
_____

SOMETHING I WANT TO REMEMBER FROM TODAY

_____
_____
_____

SOMETHING ABOUT MY FUTURE SELF IS

_____
_____
_____

YOU'LL NEVER CHANGE YOUR LIFE UNTIL YOU CHANGE SOMETHING YOU DO
DAILY. THE SECRET OF YOUR SUCCESS IS FOUND IN YOUR DAILY ROUTINE.
-JOHN C. MAXWELL

mrs.veronica anne

DAILY ALIGNMENT

MORNING

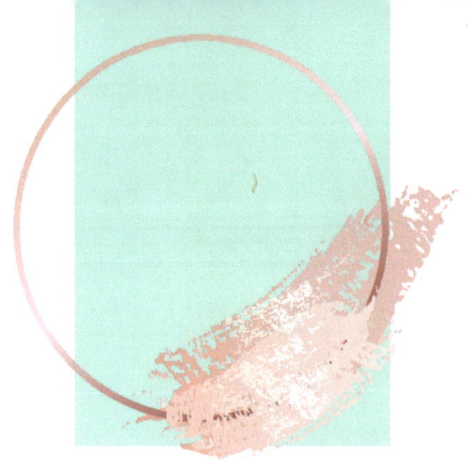

DATE TODAY:

☐ Stretch

☐ Meditate

☐ Pray

☐ Scriptures

☐ Exercise

TODAY I AM GOING
TO NOURISH MY
BODY WITH

_____

_____

_____

_____

WHAT I AM PRAYING FOR

_____

_____

_____

MEDITATION INSIGHTS

_____

_____

_____

THE SCRIPTURE I AM LETTING SINK INTO ME IS

_____

_____

_____

MY DESIGN FOR MY DAY IS

_____

_____

_____

**THE ACTION/BELIEF/PATTERN I AM WORKING TO
CHANGE IS**

_____

_____

_____

TODAY'S AFFIRMATION

DAILY ALIGNMENT

EVENING

DATE TODAY:

☐ Meditate

☐ Report back
   to God

☐ Visualize

**I FEEL GRATEFUL
FOR:**

TODAY I HONORED MYSELF BY

_____
_____

TODAY I CONNECTED WITH GOD BY

_____
_____

I SAW GOD'S HAND IN MY LIFE TODAY WHEN

_____
_____

SOMETHING I DID WELL TODAY IS

_____
_____

SOMETHING I WANT TO REMEMBER FROM TODAY

_____
_____

SOMETHING ABOUT MY FUTURE SELF IS

_____
_____

MOTIVATION IS WHAT GETS YOU STARTED.
HABIT IS WHAT KEEPS YOU GOING. -JIM ROHN

mrs.veronica anne

DAILY ALIGNMENT

MORNING

DATE TODAY:

☐ Stretch

☐ Meditate

☐ Pray

☐ Scriptures

☐ Exercise

TODAY I AM GOING
TO NOURISH MY
BODY WITH

_____

_____

_____

WHAT I AM PRAYING FOR

_____

_____

_____

MEDITATION INSIGHTS

_____

_____

_____

THE SCRIPTURE I AM LETTING SINK INTO ME IS

_____

_____

_____

MY DESIGN FOR MY DAY IS

_____

_____

_____

THE ACTION/BELIEF/PATTERN I AM WORKING TO CHANGE IS

_____

_____

_____

TODAY'S AFFIRMATION

DAILY ALIGNMENT

EVENING

DATE TODAY:

☐ Meditate

☐ Report back
   to God

☐ Visualize

**I FEEL GRATEFUL
FOR:**

TODAY I HONORED MYSELF BY

_____

_____

_____

TODAY I CONNECTED WITH GOD BY

_____

_____

_____

I SAW GOD'S HAND IN MY LIFE TODAY WHEN

_____

_____

_____

SOMETHING I DID WELL TODAY IS

_____

_____

_____

SOMETHING I WANT TO REMEMBER FROM TODAY

_____

_____

_____

SOMETHING ABOUT MY FUTURE SELF IS

_____

_____

_____

I LEARNED A LONG TIME AGO THE WISEST THING I CAN DO
IS BE ON MY OWN SIDE. - MAYA ANGELOU

"Instead of hustling to build a life that looks good, what if you slowed down and cultivated a life that feels good?"

-Erica Layne

DAILY ALIGNMENT

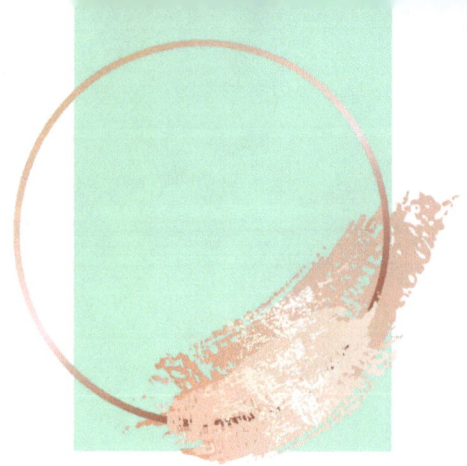

MORNING

DATE TODAY:

☐ Stretch

☐ Meditate

☐ Pray

☐ Scriptures

☐ Exercise

TODAY I AM GOING
TO NOURISH MY
BODY WITH

_____

_____

_____

WHAT I AM PRAYING FOR

_____

_____

_____

MEDITATION INSIGHTS

_____

_____

_____

THE SCRIPTURE I AM LETTING SINK INTO ME IS

_____

_____

_____

MY DESIGN FOR MY DAY IS

_____

_____

THE ACTION/BELIEF/PATTERN I AM WORKING TO CHANGE IS

_____

_____

_____

TODAY'S AFFIRMATION

DAILY ALIGNMENT

EVENING

DATE TODAY:

☐ Meditate

☐ Report back
   to God

☐ Visualize

**I FEEL GRATEFUL
FOR:**

TODAY I HONORED MYSELF BY

_____
_____
_____

TODAY I CONNECTED WITH GOD BY

_____
_____
_____

I SAW GOD'S HAND IN MY LIFE TODAY WHEN

_____
_____
_____

SOMETHING I DID WELL TODAY IS

_____
_____
_____

SOMETHING I WANT TO REMEMBER FROM TODAY

_____
_____
_____

SOMETHING ABOUT MY FUTURE SELF IS

_____
_____
_____

THE TRUTH IS THAT GOD HAS GREAT THINGS FOR YOUR LIFE. WONDERFUL
THINGS THAT ARE HEADED FOR YOU. CONTINUE TO ALIGN YOUR HEART
WITH HIS AND HANG ONTO THE PROMISES HE HAS FOR YOUR LIFE.
-LORENZO HINES

mrs.veronica anne

DAILY ALIGNMENT

MORNING

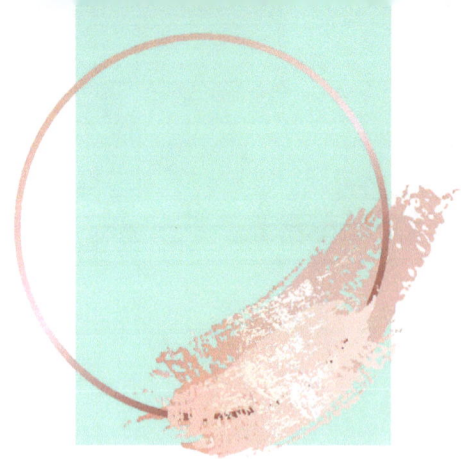

DATE TODAY:

☐ Stretch

☐ Meditate

☐ Pray

☐ Scriptures

☐ Exercise

TODAY I AM GOING
TO NOURISH MY
BODY WITH

_____

_____

_____

WHAT I AM PRAYING FOR

_____

_____

_____

MEDITATION INSIGHTS

_____

_____

_____

THE SCRIPTURE I AM LETTING SINK INTO ME IS

_____

_____

_____

MY DESIGN FOR MY DAY IS

_____

_____

_____

**THE ACTION/BELIEF/PATTERN I AM WORKING TO
CHANGE IS**

_____

_____

_____

TODAY'S AFFIRMATION

DAILY ALIGNMENT

EVENING

DATE TODAY:

☐ Meditate

☐ Report back
to God

☐ Visualize

I FEEL GRATEFUL
FOR:

TODAY I HONORED MYSELF BY

_____
_____
_____

TODAY I CONNECTED WITH GOD BY

_____
_____

I SAW GOD'S HAND IN MY LIFE TODAY WHEN

_____
_____
_____

SOMETHING I DID WELL TODAY IS

_____
_____

SOMETHING I WANT TO REMEMBER FROM TODAY

_____
_____

SOMETHING ABOUT MY FUTURE SELF IS

_____
_____
_____

YES, I AM IMPERFECT AND VULNERABLE AND SOMETIMES AFRAID. BUT
THAT DOESN'T CHANGE THE TRUTH THAT I AM ALSO BRAVE AND
WORTHY OF LOVE AND BELONGING. - BRENÉ BROWN

mrs.veronica anne

DAILY ALIGNMENT

MORNING

DATE TODAY:

- ☐ Stretch
- ☐ Meditate
- ☐ Pray
- ☐ Scriptures
- ☐ Exercise

TODAY I AM GOING
TO NOURISH MY
BODY WITH

_____

_____

_____

WHAT I AM PRAYING FOR

_____

_____

_____

MEDITATION INSIGHTS

_____

_____

_____

THE SCRIPTURE I AM LETTING SINK INTO ME IS

_____

_____

_____

MY DESIGN FOR MY DAY IS

_____

_____

_____

THE ACTION/BELIEF/PATTERN I AM WORKING TO CHANGE IS

_____

_____

_____

TODAY'S AFFIRMATION

DAILY ALIGNMENT

EVENING

DATE TODAY:

☐ Meditate

☐ Report back to God

☐ Visualize

I FEEL GRATEFUL FOR:

TODAY I HONORED MYSELF BY

_____
_____

TODAY I CONNECTED WITH GOD BY

_____
_____
_____

I SAW GOD'S HAND IN MY LIFE TODAY WHEN

_____
_____

SOMETHING I DID WELL TODAY IS

_____
_____

SOMETHING I WANT TO REMEMBER FROM TODAY

_____
_____

SOMETHING ABOUT MY FUTURE SELF IS

_____
_____
_____

TODAY IS THE OPPORTUNITY TO BUILD THE TOMORROW YOU WANT. - KEN POIROT

mrs.veronica anne

DAILY ALIGNMENT

MORNING

DATE TODAY:

☐ Stretch

☐ Meditate

☐ Pray

☐ Scriptures

☐ Exercise

WHAT I AM PRAYING FOR

_____
_____
_____

MEDITATION INSIGHTS

_____
_____
_____

THE SCRIPTURE I AM LETTING SINK INTO ME IS

_____
_____
_____

TODAY I AM GOING
TO NOURISH MY
BODY WITH

MY DESIGN FOR MY DAY IS

_____
_____
_____

_____
_____

THE ACTION/BELIEF/PATTERN I AM WORKING TO CHANGE IS

_____
_____
_____

TODAY'S AFFIRMATION

DAILY ALIGNMENT

EVENING

DATE TODAY:

☐ Meditate

☐ Report back
   to God

☐ Visualize

**I FEEL GRATEFUL
FOR:**

TODAY I HONORED MYSELF BY

_____
_____
_____

TODAY I CONNECTED WITH GOD BY

_____
_____
_____

I SAW GOD'S HAND IN MY LIFE TODAY WHEN

_____
_____
_____

SOMETHING I DID WELL TODAY IS

_____
_____
_____

SOMETHING I WANT TO REMEMBER FROM TODAY

_____
_____
_____

SOMETHING ABOUT MY FUTURE SELF IS

_____
_____
_____

YOU CAN'T DO ANYTHING ABOUT THE LENGTH OF YOUR LIFE, BUT YOU
CAN DO SOMETHING ABOUT IT'S WIDTH AND DEPTH.
-ATTRIBUTED TO H.L. MENCKEN."

mrs.veronica anne

God is within her.
She will not fall.

-Psalm 46:5

DAILY ALIGNMENT

MORNING

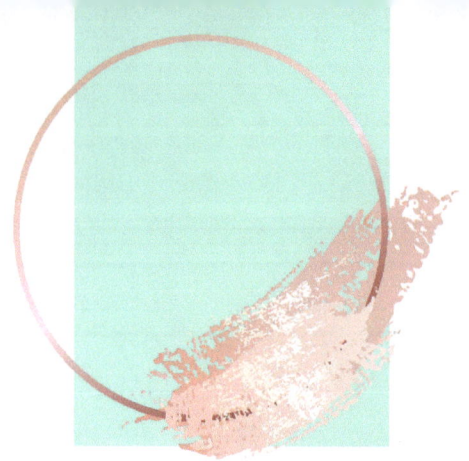

DATE TODAY:

☐ Stretch

☐ Meditate

☐ Pray

☐ Scriptures

☐ Exercise

TODAY I AM GOING
TO NOURISH MY
BODY WITH

_____

_____

_____

WHAT I AM PRAYING FOR

_____

_____

_____

MEDITATION INSIGHTS

_____

_____

_____

THE SCRIPTURE I AM LETTING SINK INTO ME IS

_____

_____

_____

MY DESIGN FOR MY DAY IS

_____

_____

**THE ACTION/BELIEF/PATTERN I AM WORKING TO
CHANGE IS**

_____

_____

_____

TODAY'S AFFIRMATION

DAILY ALIGNMENT

EVENING

DATE TODAY:

☐ Meditate

☐ Report back to God

☐ Visualize

I FEEL GRATEFUL FOR:

TODAY I HONORED MYSELF BY

_____

_____

TODAY I CONNECTED WITH GOD BY

_____

_____

I SAW GOD'S HAND IN MY LIFE TODAY WHEN

_____

_____

SOMETHING I DID WELL TODAY IS

_____

_____

SOMETHING I WANT TO REMEMBER FROM TODAY

_____

_____

SOMETHING ABOUT MY FUTURE SELF IS

_____

_____

IF YOUR DREAMS DON'T SCARE YOU, THEY ARE TOO SMALL.
- RICHARD BRANSON

mrs.veronica anne

DAILY ALIGNMENT

MORNING

DATE TODAY:

☐ Stretch

☐ Meditate

☐ Pray

☐ Scriptures

☐ Exercise

TODAY I AM GOING
TO NOURISH MY
BODY WITH

_____

_____

_____

WHAT I AM PRAYING FOR

_____

_____

_____

MEDITATION INSIGHTS

_____

_____

_____

THE SCRIPTURE I AM LETTING SINK INTO ME IS

_____

_____

_____

MY DESIGN FOR MY DAY IS

_____

_____

THE ACTION/BELIEF/PATTERN I AM WORKING TO CHANGE IS

_____

_____

_____

TODAY'S AFFIRMATION

DAILY ALIGNMENT

EVENING

DATE TODAY:

☐ Meditate

☐ Report back
  to God

☐ Visualize

**I FEEL GRATEFUL
FOR:**

TODAY I HONORED MYSELF BY

_____
_____
_____

TODAY I CONNECTED WITH GOD BY

_____
_____
_____

I SAW GOD'S HAND IN MY LIFE TODAY WHEN

_____
_____
_____

SOMETHING I DID WELL TODAY IS

_____
_____
_____

SOMETHING I WANT TO REMEMBER FROM TODAY

_____
_____
_____

SOMETHING ABOUT MY FUTURE SELF IS

_____
_____
_____

I WILL NOT LET ANYONE WALK THROUGH MY MIND
WITH THEIR DIRTY FEET.-MAHATMA GANDHI

mrs.veronica anne

DAILY ALIGNMENT

MORNING

DATE TODAY:

☐ Stretch

☐ Meditate

☐ Pray

☐ Scriptures

☐ Exercise

TODAY I AM GOING
TO NOURISH MY
BODY WITH

_____

_____

_____

_____

WHAT I AM PRAYING FOR

_____

_____

_____

MEDITATION INSIGHTS

_____

_____

_____

THE SCRIPTURE I AM LETTING SINK INTO ME IS

_____

_____

_____

MY DESIGN FOR MY DAY IS

_____

_____

_____

THE ACTION/BELIEF/PATTERN I AM WORKING TO CHANGE IS

_____

_____

_____

TODAY'S AFFIRMATION

DAILY ALIGNMENT

EVENING

DATE TODAY:

☐ Meditate

☐ Report back to God

☐ Visualize

I FEEL GRATEFUL FOR:

TODAY I HONORED MYSELF BY

_____
_____

TODAY I CONNECTED WITH GOD BY

_____
_____

I SAW GOD'S HAND IN MY LIFE TODAY WHEN

_____
_____

SOMETHING I DID WELL TODAY IS

_____
_____

SOMETHING I WANT TO REMEMBER FROM TODAY

_____
_____

SOMETHING ABOUT MY FUTURE SELF IS

_____
_____

EVERY ACTION YOU TAKE IS A VOTE FOR THE PERSON YOU
WISH TO BECOME. -JAMES CLEAR

DAILY ALIGNMENT

MORNING

DATE TODAY:

☐ Stretch

☐ Meditate

☐ Pray

☐ Scriptures

☐ Exercise

TODAY I AM GOING
TO NOURISH MY
BODY WITH

_____

_____

_____

WHAT I AM PRAYING FOR

_____

_____

MEDITATION INSIGHTS

_____

_____

THE SCRIPTURE I AM LETTING SINK INTO ME IS

_____

_____

_____

MY DESIGN FOR MY DAY IS

_____

_____

**THE ACTION/BELIEF/PATTERN I AM WORKING TO
CHANGE IS**

_____

_____

_____

TODAY'S AFFIRMATION

DAILY ALIGNMENT

EVENING

DATE TODAY:

☐ Meditate

☐ Report back
   to God

☐ Visualize

**I FEEL GRATEFUL
FOR:**

TODAY I HONORED MYSELF BY

_____
_____
_____

TODAY I CONNECTED WITH GOD BY

_____
_____
_____

I SAW GOD'S HAND IN MY LIFE TODAY WHEN

_____
_____
_____

SOMETHING I DID WELL TODAY IS

_____
_____
_____

SOMETHING I WANT TO REMEMBER FROM TODAY

_____
_____

SOMETHING ABOUT MY FUTURE SELF IS

_____
_____
_____

SHE REMEMBERED WHO SHE WAS AND THE GAME CHANGED.
-LALAH DELIA

mrs.veronica anne

When you choose
to follow Christ,
you choose to be
changed

-Ezra Taft Benson

DAILY ALIGNMENT

MORNING

DATE TODAY:

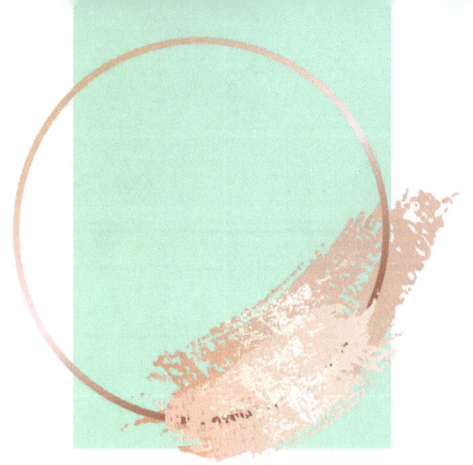

☐ Stretch

☐ Meditate

☐ Pray

☐ Scriptures

☐ Exercise

TODAY I AM GOING
TO NOURISH MY
BODY WITH

_____
_____
_____
_____

WHAT I AM PRAYING FOR

_____
_____
_____

MEDITATION INSIGHTS

_____
_____
_____

THE SCRIPTURE I AM LETTING SINK INTO ME IS

_____
_____
_____

MY DESIGN FOR MY DAY IS

_____
_____
_____

**THE ACTION/BELIEF/PATTERN I AM WORKING TO
CHANGE IS**

_____
_____
_____

TODAY'S AFFIRMATION

DAILY ALIGNMENT

EVENING

DATE TODAY:

☐ Meditate

☐ Report back to God

☐ Visualize

I FEEL GRATEFUL FOR:

TODAY I HONORED MYSELF BY

_____
_____

TODAY I CONNECTED WITH GOD BY

_____
_____

I SAW GOD'S HAND IN MY LIFE TODAY WHEN

_____
_____

SOMETHING I DID WELL TODAY IS

_____
_____

SOMETHING I WANT TO REMEMBER FROM TODAY

_____
_____

SOMETHING ABOUT MY FUTURE SELF IS

_____
_____

GIVE YOURSELF PERMISSION TO LET GO OF OTHER PEOPLE'S OPINIONS OF YOU, -CAITLIN BACHER

mrs.veronica anne

DAILY ALIGNMENT

MORNING

DATE TODAY:

☐ Stretch

☐ Meditate

☐ Pray

☐ Scriptures

☐ Exercise

TODAY I AM GOING
TO NOURISH MY
BODY WITH

_____

_____

_____

WHAT I AM PRAYING FOR

_____

_____

_____

MEDITATION INSIGHTS

_____

_____

_____

THE SCRIPTURE I AM LETTING SINK INTO ME IS

_____

_____

_____

MY DESIGN FOR MY DAY IS

_____

_____

_____

THE ACTION/BELIEF/PATTERN I AM WORKING TO CHANGE IS

_____

_____

_____

TODAY'S AFFIRMATION

DAILY ALIGNMENT

EVENING

DATE TODAY:

☐ Meditate

☐ Report back
   to God

☐ Visualize

**I FEEL GRATEFUL
FOR:**

TODAY I HONORED MYSELF BY

_____
_____
_____

TODAY I CONNECTED WITH GOD BY

_____
_____
_____

I SAW GOD'S HAND IN MY LIFE TODAY WHEN

_____
_____
_____

SOMETHING I DID WELL TODAY IS

_____
_____

SOMETHING I WANT TO REMEMBER FROM TODAY

_____
_____

SOMETHING ABOUT MY FUTURE SELF IS

_____
_____
_____

WALK LIKE YOU HAVE 3,000 ANCESTORS WALKING BEHIND YOU.
-AFRICAN PROVERB

mrs.veronica anne

DAILY ALIGNMENT

MORNING

DATE TODAY:

☐ Stretch

☐ Meditate

☐ Pray

☐ Scriptures

☐ Exercise

TODAY I AM GOING
TO NOURISH MY
BODY WITH

_____

_____

_____

WHAT I AM PRAYING FOR

_____

_____

MEDITATION INSIGHTS

_____

_____

THE SCRIPTURE I AM LETTING SINK INTO ME IS

_____

_____

_____

MY DESIGN FOR MY DAY IS

_____

_____

THE ACTION/BELIEF/PATTERN I AM WORKING TO CHANGE IS

_____

_____

_____

TODAY'S AFFIRMATION

DAILY ALIGNMENT

EVENING

DATE TODAY:

☐ Meditate

☐ Report back to God

☐ Visualize

I FEEL GRATEFUL FOR:

TODAY I HONORED MYSELF BY

_____
_____
_____

TODAY I CONNECTED WITH GOD BY

_____
_____
_____

I SAW GOD'S HAND IN MY LIFE TODAY WHEN

_____
_____
_____

SOMETHING I DID WELL TODAY IS

_____
_____
_____

SOMETHING I WANT TO REMEMBER FROM TODAY

_____
_____
_____

SOMETHING ABOUT MY FUTURE SELF IS

_____
_____
_____

YOUR CHALLENGES ARE NOT AN INDICTMENT AGAINST YOUR CAPACITY.
- PRISCILLA SHIRER

mrs.veronica anne

DAILY ALIGNMENT

MORNING

DATE TODAY:

☐ Stretch

☐ Meditate

☐ Pray

☐ Scriptures

☐ Exercise

TODAY I AM GOING
TO NOURISH MY
BODY WITH

_____

_____

_____

WHAT I AM PRAYING FOR

_____

_____

_____

MEDITATION INSIGHTS

_____

_____

_____

THE SCRIPTURE I AM LETTING SINK INTO ME IS

_____

_____

_____

MY DESIGN FOR MY DAY IS

_____

_____

_____

THE ACTION/BELIEF/PATTERN I AM WORKING TO CHANGE IS

_____

_____

_____

TODAY'S AFFIRMATION

DAILY ALIGNMENT

EVENING

DATE TODAY:

☐ Meditate

☐ Report back
to God

☐ Visualize

**I FEEL GRATEFUL
FOR:**

TODAY I HONORED MYSELF BY

_____
_____

TODAY I CONNECTED WITH GOD BY

_____
_____

I SAW GOD'S HAND IN MY LIFE TODAY WHEN

_____
_____

SOMETHING I DID WELL TODAY IS

_____
_____

SOMETHING I WANT TO REMEMBER FROM TODAY

_____
_____

SOMETHING ABOUT MY FUTURE SELF IS

_____
_____

THE GREATEST STEP TOWARDS A LIFE OF HAPPINESS AND SIMPLICITY IS
TO LET GO. TRUST IN THE POWER THAT IS ALREADY TAKING CARE OF
YOU SPONTANEOUSLY WITHOUT EFFORT. -MOOJI

mrs.veronica anne

I have confidence
in me because
I have confidence in
Him

-Veronica Rogers

DAILY ALIGNMENT

MORNING

DATE TODAY:

☐ Stretch

☐ Meditate

☐ Pray

☐ Scriptures

☐ Exercise

TODAY I AM GOING
TO NOURISH MY
BODY WITH

_____

_____

_____

WHAT I AM PRAYING FOR

_____

_____

_____

MEDITATION INSIGHTS

_____

_____

_____

THE SCRIPTURE I AM LETTING SINK INTO ME IS

_____

_____

_____

MY DESIGN FOR MY DAY IS

_____

_____

THE ACTION/BELIEF/PATTERN I AM WORKING TO CHANGE IS

_____

_____

_____

TODAY'S AFFIRMATION

DAILY ALIGNMENT

EVENING

DATE TODAY:

☐ Meditate

☐ Report back
to God

☐ Visualize

**I FEEL GRATEFUL
FOR:**

TODAY I HONORED MYSELF BY

_____

_____

_____

TODAY I CONNECTED WITH GOD BY

_____

_____

I SAW GOD'S HAND IN MY LIFE TODAY WHEN

_____

_____

_____

SOMETHING I DID WELL TODAY IS

_____

_____

SOMETHING I WANT TO REMEMBER FROM TODAY

_____

_____

SOMETHING ABOUT MY FUTURE SELF IS

_____

_____

_____

NEEDING APPROVAL IS TANTAMOUNT TO SAYING 'YOUR VIEW OF ME IS
MORE IMPORTANT THAN MY OWN OPINION OF MYSELF.' - WAYNE DYER

mrs.veronica anne

DAILY ALIGNMENT

MORNING

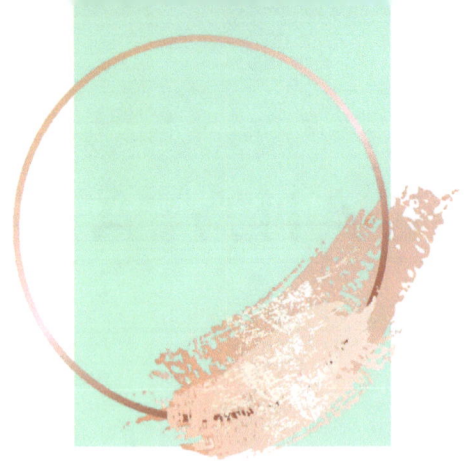

DATE TODAY:

☐ Stretch

☐ Meditate

☐ Pray

☐ Scriptures

☐ Exercise

TODAY I AM GOING
TO NOURISH MY
BODY WITH

_____

_____

_____

WHAT I AM PRAYING FOR

_____

_____

MEDITATION INSIGHTS

_____

_____

THE SCRIPTURE I AM LETTING SINK INTO ME IS

_____

_____

_____

MY DESIGN FOR MY DAY IS

_____

_____

THE ACTION/BELIEF/PATTERN I AM WORKING TO CHANGE IS

_____

_____

_____

TODAY'S AFFIRMATION

DAILY ALIGNMENT

EVENING

DATE TODAY:

☐ Meditate

☐ Report back
  to God

☐ Visualize

I FEEL GRATEFUL FOR:

TODAY I HONORED MYSELF BY

_____
_____
_____

TODAY I CONNECTED WITH GOD BY

_____
_____
_____

I SAW GOD'S HAND IN MY LIFE TODAY WHEN

_____
_____
_____

SOMETHING I DID WELL TODAY IS

_____
_____
_____

SOMETHING I WANT TO REMEMBER FROM TODAY

_____
_____
_____

SOMETHING ABOUT MY FUTURE SELF IS

_____
_____
_____

IT TAKES YEARS AS A WOMAN TO UNLEARN WHAT YOU HAVE BEEN
TAUGHT TO BE SORRY FOR. - AMY POEHLER

DAILY ALIGNMENT

MORNING

DATE TODAY:

☐ Stretch

☐ Meditate

☐ Pray

☐ Scriptures

☐ Exercise

TODAY I AM GOING
TO NOURISH MY
BODY WITH

_____
_____
_____

WHAT I AM PRAYING FOR

_____
_____
_____

MEDITATION INSIGHTS

_____
_____
_____

THE SCRIPTURE I AM LETTING SINK INTO ME IS

_____
_____
_____

MY DESIGN FOR MY DAY IS

_____
_____
_____

THE ACTION/BELIEF/PATTERN I AM WORKING TO CHANGE IS

_____
_____
_____

TODAY'S AFFIRMATION

DAILY ALIGNMENT

EVENING

DATE TODAY:

☐ Meditate

☐ Report back to God

☐ Visualize

I FEEL GRATEFUL FOR:

TODAY I HONORED MYSELF BY

_____
_____
_____

TODAY I CONNECTED WITH GOD BY

_____
_____
_____

I SAW GOD'S HAND IN MY LIFE TODAY WHEN

_____
_____
_____

SOMETHING I DID WELL TODAY IS

_____
_____
_____

SOMETHING I WANT TO REMEMBER FROM TODAY

_____
_____

SOMETHING ABOUT MY FUTURE SELF IS

_____
_____
_____

I AM OPEN TO MY LIFE BEING BETTER THAN MY IMAGINATION
-LIANA NAIMA

mrs.veronica anne

DAILY ALIGNMENT

MORNING

DATE TODAY:

☐ Stretch

☐ Meditate

☐ Pray

☐ Scriptures

☐ Exercise

TODAY I AM GOING
TO NOURISH MY
BODY WITH

_____

_____

_____

_____

WHAT I AM PRAYING FOR

_____

_____

_____

MEDITATION INSIGHTS

_____

_____

_____

THE SCRIPTURE I AM LETTING SINK INTO ME IS

_____

_____

_____

MY DESIGN FOR MY DAY IS

_____

_____

_____

THE ACTION/BELIEF/PATTERN I AM WORKING TO CHANGE IS

_____

_____

_____

TODAY'S AFFIRMATION

DAILY ALIGNMENT

EVENING

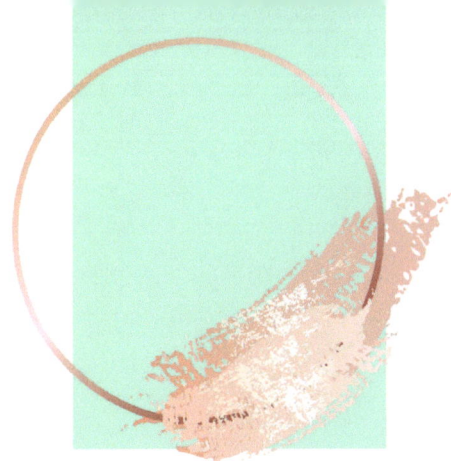

DATE TODAY:

☐   Meditate

☐   Report back
      to God

☐   Visualize

**I FEEL GRATEFUL
FOR:**

TODAY I HONORED MYSELF BY

_____

_____

TODAY I CONNECTED WITH GOD BY

_____

_____

I SAW GOD'S HAND IN MY LIFE TODAY WHEN

_____

_____

SOMETHING I DID WELL TODAY IS

_____

_____

SOMETHING I WANT TO REMEMBER FROM TODAY

_____

_____

SOMETHING ABOUT MY FUTURE SELF IS

_____

_____

_____

I LOVE THE PERSON I'VE BECOME BECAUSE I FOUGHT TO BECOME HER.
- KACI DIANE

Please don't shrink
yourself to make
someone else feel
more comfortable.
Love would never
ask that of you

-Veronica Rogers

DAILY ALIGNMENT

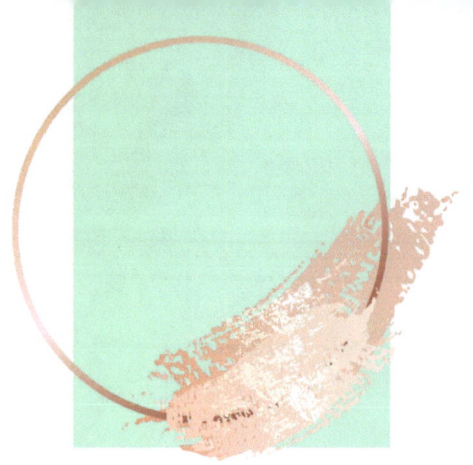

MORNING

DATE TODAY:

☐ Stretch

☐ Meditate

☐ Pray

☐ Scriptures

☐ Exercise

TODAY I AM GOING
TO NOURISH MY
BODY WITH

_____

_____

_____

WHAT I AM PRAYING FOR

_____

_____

MEDITATION INSIGHTS

_____

_____

THE SCRIPTURE I AM LETTING SINK INTO ME IS

_____

_____

_____

MY DESIGN FOR MY DAY IS

_____

_____

THE ACTION/BELIEF/PATTERN I AM WORKING TO CHANGE IS

_____

_____

_____

TODAY'S AFFIRMATION

DAILY ALIGNMENT

EVENING

DATE TODAY:

☐ Meditate

☐ Report back
   to God

☐ Visualize

**I FEEL GRATEFUL
FOR:**

TODAY I HONORED MYSELF BY

_____
_____
_____

TODAY I CONNECTED WITH GOD BY

_____
_____
_____

I SAW GOD'S HAND IN MY LIFE TODAY WHEN

_____
_____
_____

SOMETHING I DID WELL TODAY IS

_____
_____
_____

SOMETHING I WANT TO REMEMBER FROM TODAY

_____
_____
_____

SOMETHING ABOUT MY FUTURE SELF IS

_____
_____
_____

WHEN YOU BEGIN TO CATCH EVEN A GLIMPSE OF HOW HEAVENLY
FATHER SEES YOU AND WHAT HE IS COUNTING ON YOU TO DO FOR HIM,
YOUR LIFE WILL NEVER BE THE SAME. -RUSSELL M. NELSON

mrs.veronica anne

DAILY ALIGNMENT

MORNING

DATE TODAY:

☐ Stretch

☐ Meditate

☐ Pray

☐ Scriptures

☐ Exercise

TODAY I AM GOING
TO NOURISH MY
BODY WITH

_____

_____

_____

_____

WHAT I AM PRAYING FOR

_____

_____

_____

MEDITATION INSIGHTS

_____

_____

_____

THE SCRIPTURE I AM LETTING SINK INTO ME IS

_____

_____

_____

MY DESIGN FOR MY DAY IS

_____

_____

THE ACTION/BELIEF/PATTERN I AM WORKING TO CHANGE IS

_____

_____

_____

TODAY'S AFFIRMATION

DAILY ALIGNMENT

EVENING

DATE TODAY:

☐ Meditate

☐ Report back
   to God

☐ Visualize

**I FEEL GRATEFUL
FOR:**

TODAY I HONORED MYSELF BY

_____
_____

TODAY I CONNECTED WITH GOD BY

_____
_____

I SAW GOD'S HAND IN MY LIFE TODAY WHEN

_____
_____

SOMETHING I DID WELL TODAY IS

_____
_____

SOMETHING I WANT TO REMEMBER FROM TODAY

_____
_____

SOMETHING ABOUT MY FUTURE SELF IS

_____
_____

I HAVE ALREADY SETTLED IT FOR MYSELF, SO FLATTERY AND CRITICISM
GO DOWN THE SAME DRAIN AND I AM QUITE FREE. -GEORGIA O'KEEFE

DAILY ALIGNMENT

MORNING

DATE TODAY:

☐ Stretch

☐ Meditate

☐ Pray

☐ Scriptures

☐ Exercise

WHAT I AM PRAYING FOR

_____
_____
_____

MEDITATION INSIGHTS

_____
_____
_____

THE SCRIPTURE I AM LETTING SINK INTO ME IS

_____
_____
_____

TODAY I AM GOING
TO NOURISH MY
BODY WITH

_____

_____

_____

MY DESIGN FOR MY DAY IS

_____
_____
_____

THE ACTION/BELIEF/PATTERN I AM WORKING TO
CHANGE IS

_____
_____
_____

TODAY'S AFFIRMATION

DAILY ALIGNMENT

EVENING

DATE TODAY:

☐ Meditate

☐ Report back to God

☐ Visualize

I FEEL GRATEFUL FOR:

TODAY I HONORED MYSELF BY

_____

_____

TODAY I CONNECTED WITH GOD BY

_____

_____

I SAW GOD'S HAND IN MY LIFE TODAY WHEN

_____

_____

SOMETHING I DID WELL TODAY IS

_____

_____

SOMETHING I WANT TO REMEMBER FROM TODAY

_____

_____

SOMETHING ABOUT MY FUTURE SELF IS

_____

_____

GOD GENEROUSLY MANIFESTS TO US THOSE THINGS WE ARE SEEKING - JUST AS SOON AS HE PERCEIVES WE ARE READY. -WENDY NELSON

DAILY ALIGNMENT

MORNING

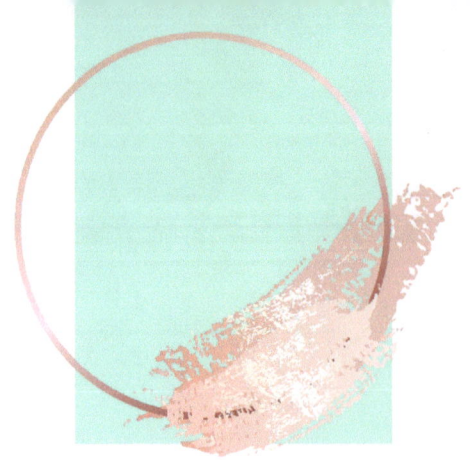

DATE TODAY:

☐ Stretch

☐ Meditate

☐ Pray

☐ Scriptures

☐ Exercise

TODAY I AM GOING
TO NOURISH MY
BODY WITH

_____

_____

_____

WHAT I AM PRAYING FOR

_____

_____

_____

MEDITATION INSIGHTS

_____

_____

_____

THE SCRIPTURE I AM LETTING SINK INTO ME IS

_____

_____

_____

MY DESIGN FOR MY DAY IS

_____

_____

_____

THE ACTION/BELIEF/PATTERN I AM WORKING TO CHANGE IS

_____

_____

_____

TODAY'S AFFIRMATION

DAILY ALIGNMENT

EVENING

DATE TODAY:

☐ Meditate

☐ Report back to God

☐ Visualize

I FEEL GRATEFUL FOR:

TODAY I HONORED MYSELF BY

_____
_____

TODAY I CONNECTED WITH GOD BY

_____
_____

I SAW GOD'S HAND IN MY LIFE TODAY WHEN

_____
_____

SOMETHING I DID WELL TODAY IS

_____
_____

SOMETHING I WANT TO REMEMBER FROM TODAY

_____
_____

SOMETHING ABOUT MY FUTURE SELF IS

_____
_____

IT HAS NEVER BEEN MORE IMPERATIVE TO KNOW HOW THE SPIRIT SPEAKS TO YOU THAN RIGHT NOW. . . DO WHATEVER IT TAKES TO INCREASE YOUR SPIRITUAL CAPACITY TO RECEIVE PERSONAL REVELATION.
-RUSSELL M. NELSON

mrs.veronica anne

If you have things that you are trying to master on your own, why are you doing that? He is ready to help you Now. He is waiting for you to bring your troubles to Him. Tap into His grace, allow Him to change you, become a new person.
-Veronica Rogers

DAILY ALIGNMENT

MORNING

DATE TODAY:

☐ Stretch

☐ Meditate

☐ Pray

☐ Scriptures

☐ Exercise

WHAT I AM PRAYING FOR

_____
_____
_____

MEDITATION INSIGHTS

_____
_____
_____

THE SCRIPTURE I AM LETTING SINK INTO ME IS

_____
_____
_____

TODAY I AM GOING
TO NOURISH MY
BODY WITH

_____

_____

_____

_____

MY DESIGN FOR MY DAY IS

_____
_____
_____

THE ACTION/BELIEF/PATTERN I AM WORKING TO CHANGE IS

_____
_____
_____

TODAY'S AFFIRMATION

DAILY ALIGNMENT

EVENING

DATE TODAY:

☐ Meditate

☐ Report back to God

☐ Visualize

I FEEL GRATEFUL FOR:

TODAY I HONORED MYSELF BY

_____

_____

TODAY I CONNECTED WITH GOD BY

_____

_____

I SAW GOD'S HAND IN MY LIFE TODAY WHEN

_____

_____

SOMETHING I DID WELL TODAY IS

_____

_____

SOMETHING I WANT TO REMEMBER FROM TODAY

_____

_____

SOMETHING ABOUT MY FUTURE SELF IS

_____

_____

_____

THE SURRENDER OF OUR WILL TO GOD'S WILL IS, IN FACT, NOT SURRENDER
AT ALL, BUT THE BEGINNING OF A GLORIOUS VICTORY.
-NEIL L. ANDERSON

mrs.veronica anne

DAILY ALIGNMENT

MORNING

DATE TODAY:

☐ Stretch

☐ Meditate

☐ Pray

☐ Scriptures

☐ Exercise

WHAT I AM PRAYING FOR

_____
_____
_____

MEDITATION INSIGHTS

_____
_____
_____

THE SCRIPTURE I AM LETTING SINK INTO ME IS

_____
_____
_____

TODAY I AM GOING
TO NOURISH MY
BODY WITH

MY DESIGN FOR MY DAY IS

_____
_____

_____
_____
_____
_____

THE ACTION/BELIEF/PATTERN I AM WORKING TO CHANGE IS

_____
_____
_____

TODAY'S AFFIRMATION

DAILY ALIGNMENT

EVENING

DATE TODAY:

☐ Meditate

☐ Report back
   to God

☐ Visualize

**I FEEL GRATEFUL
FOR:**

TODAY I HONORED MYSELF BY

_____
_____
_____

TODAY I CONNECTED WITH GOD BY

_____
_____

I SAW GOD'S HAND IN MY LIFE TODAY WHEN

_____
_____
_____

SOMETHING I DID WELL TODAY IS

_____
_____
_____

SOMETHING I WANT TO REMEMBER FROM TODAY

_____
_____

SOMETHING ABOUT MY FUTURE SELF IS

_____
_____
_____

LOOK CLOSELY AT THE PRESENT YOU ARE CONSTRUCTING. IT SHOULD
LOOK LIKE THE FUTURE YOU ARE DREAMING, - ALICE WALKER

mrs.veronica anne

Free Flow

Any thoughts, quotes, or journaling you need room for

FREE FLOW

Any thoughts, quotes, or journaling you need room for

Free Flow

Any thoughts, quotes, or journaling you need room for

FREE FLOW

Any thoughts, quotes, or journaling you need room for

FREE FLOW

Any thoughts, quotes, or journaling you need room for

Free Flow

Any thoughts, quotes, or journaling you need room for

FREE FLOW

Any thoughts, quotes, or journaling you need room for

Free Flow

Any thoughts, quotes, or journaling you need room for

Allow yourself to dream big. To want things that are not quite within reach. To have a totally different life than the one you have right now. To change. To grow. To be who you were meant to be.
-Veronica Rogers

About the Author

Veronica is an author and meditation teacher, among other things. Having eliminated her own post-traumatic stress disorder, depression, and anxiety, she focuses on helping others heal and better connect with God. When she is not creating, she is reading her ever-growing stack of books and loves learning how to do new things.

She has three adult children and lives in Eastern Arizona with her husband and two daughters.

Learn more about Veronica at mrsveronicaanne.com

Feel free to share your experience with this workbook on Instagram. Take a photo and tag @mrs.veronica.anne

www.ingramcontent.com/pod-product-compliance
Lightning Source LLC
Chambersburg PA
CBHW041431090426
42744CB00003B/29